# MINDFULNESS

NAME: _____

DATE: _____

I CAN DO THIS

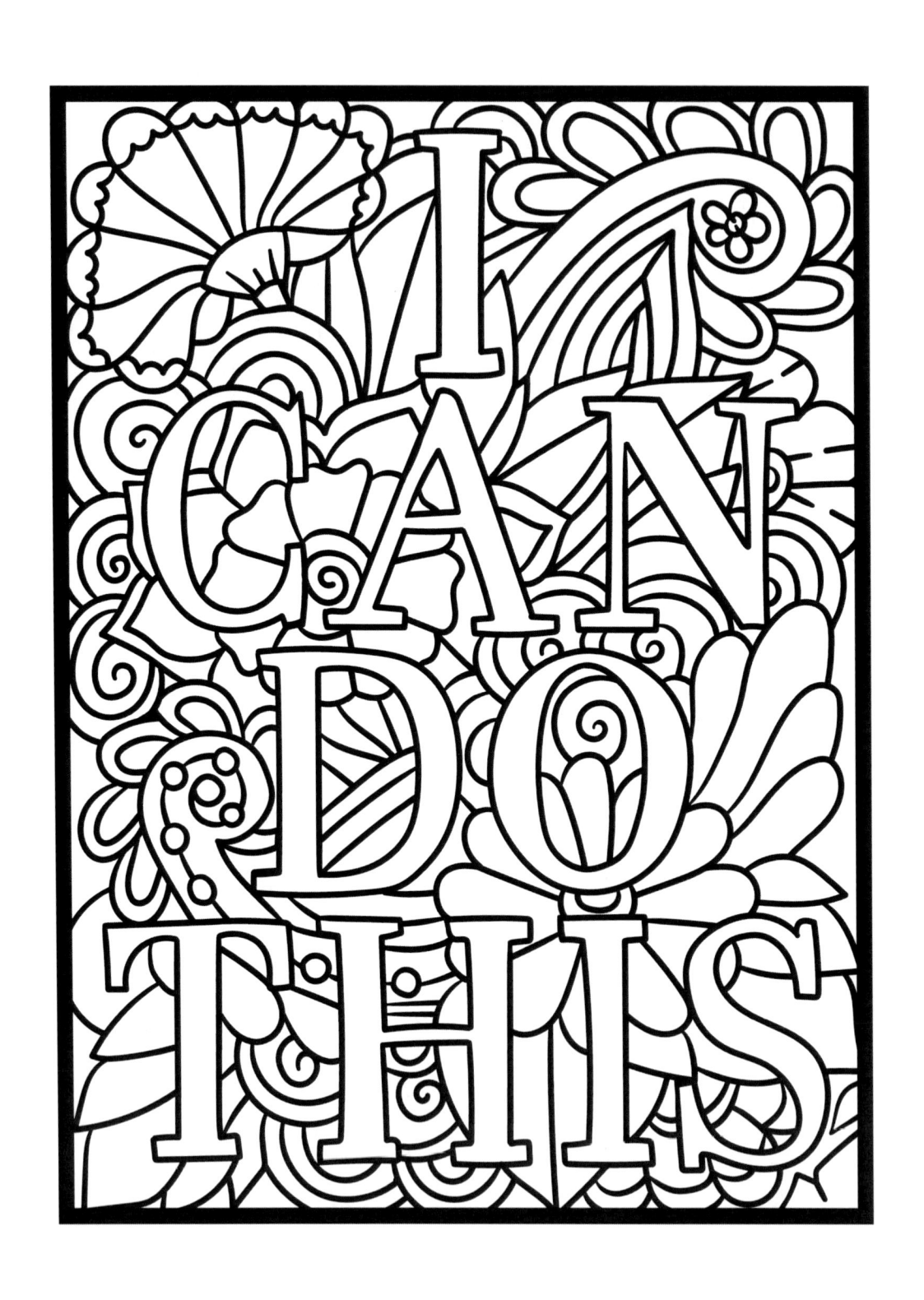

Thankful
GRATEFUL
BLESSED

# Life is full of Possibilities

Stop Dreaming Start Doing

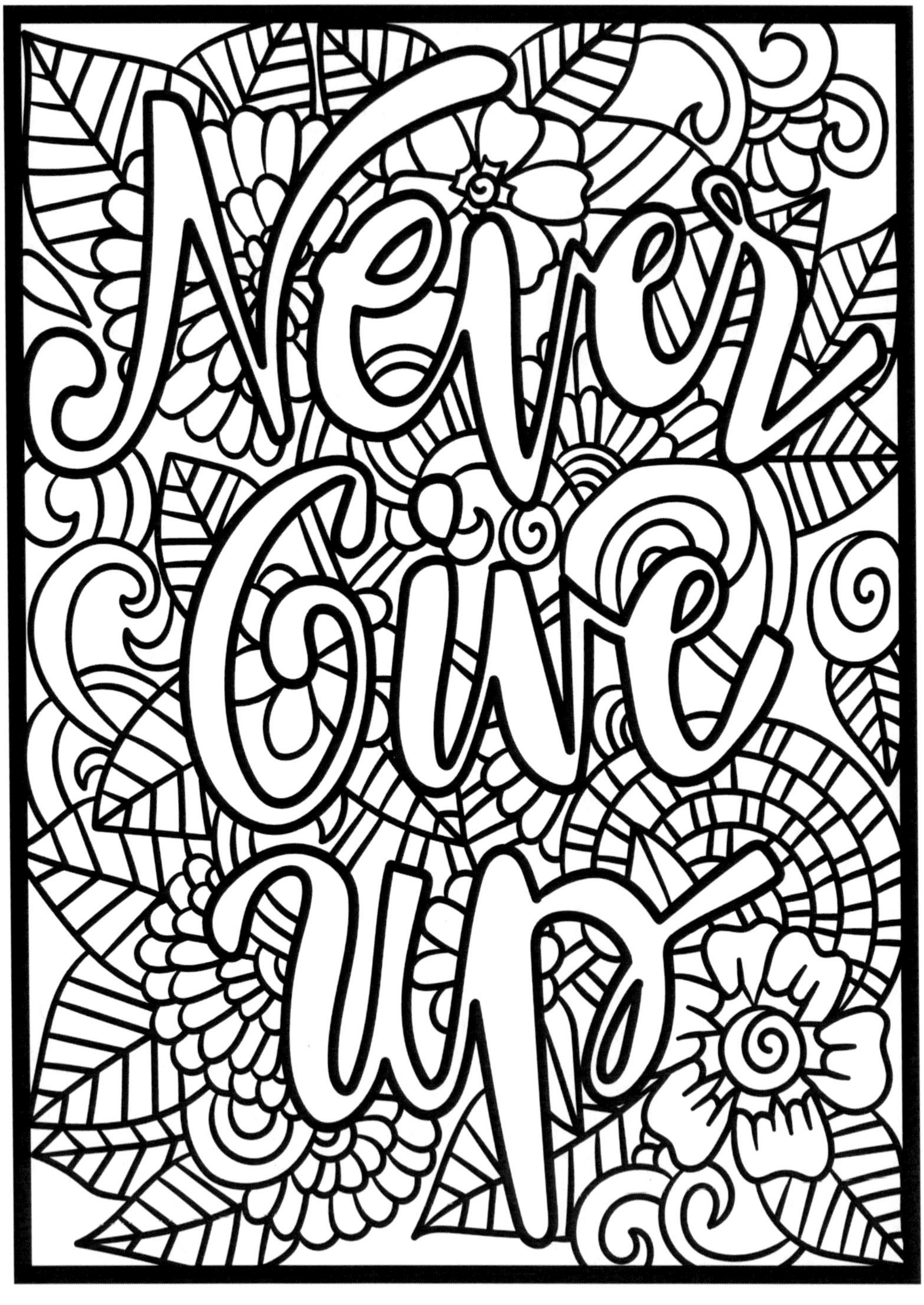
Never Give up

LIVE LAUGH LOVE

LIVE your DREAM

EVERY DAY IS A FRESH START

OLD WAYS WON'T OPEN NEW DOORS

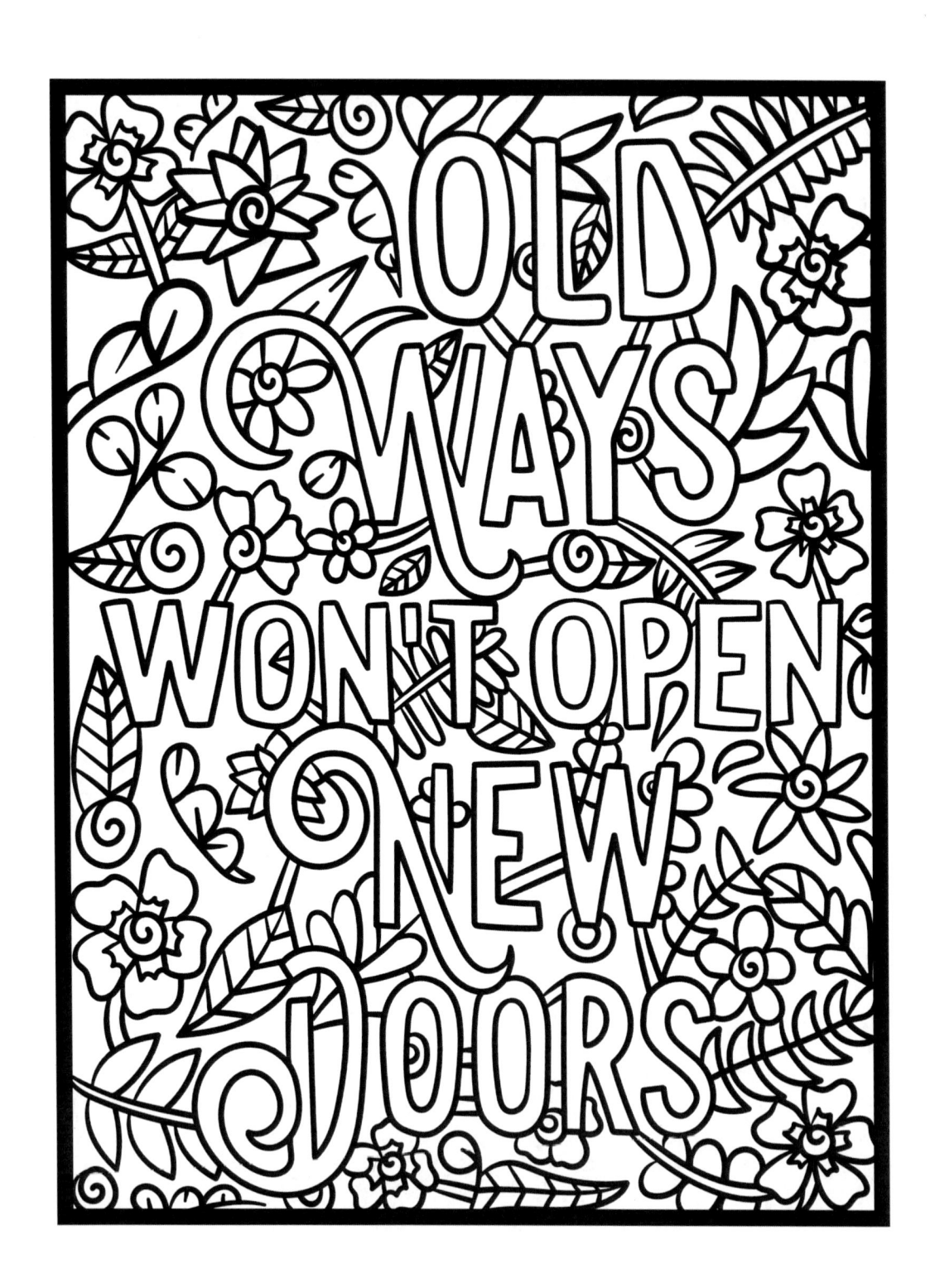

GOOD things take time

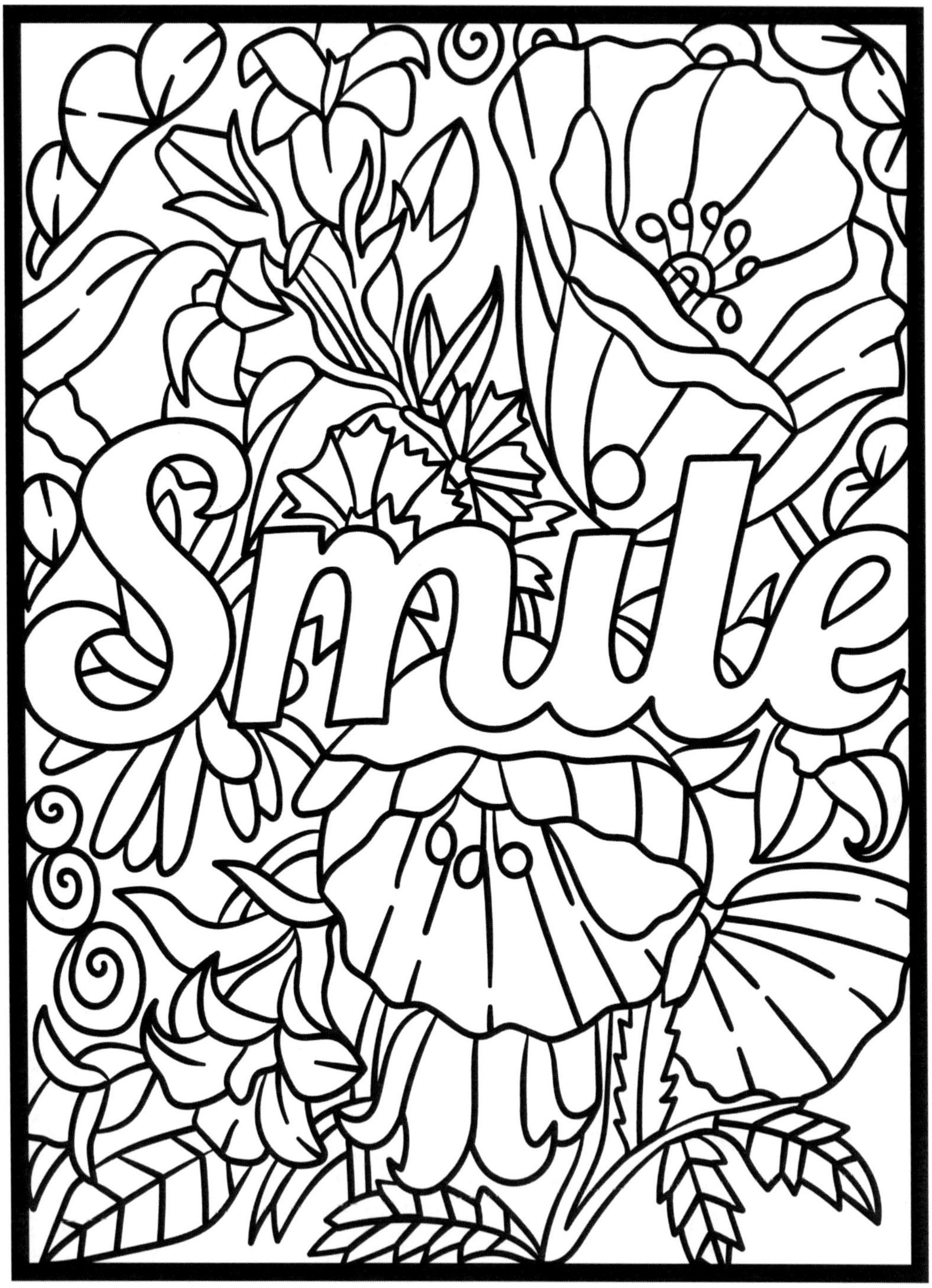
Smile

Life is tough but so you are

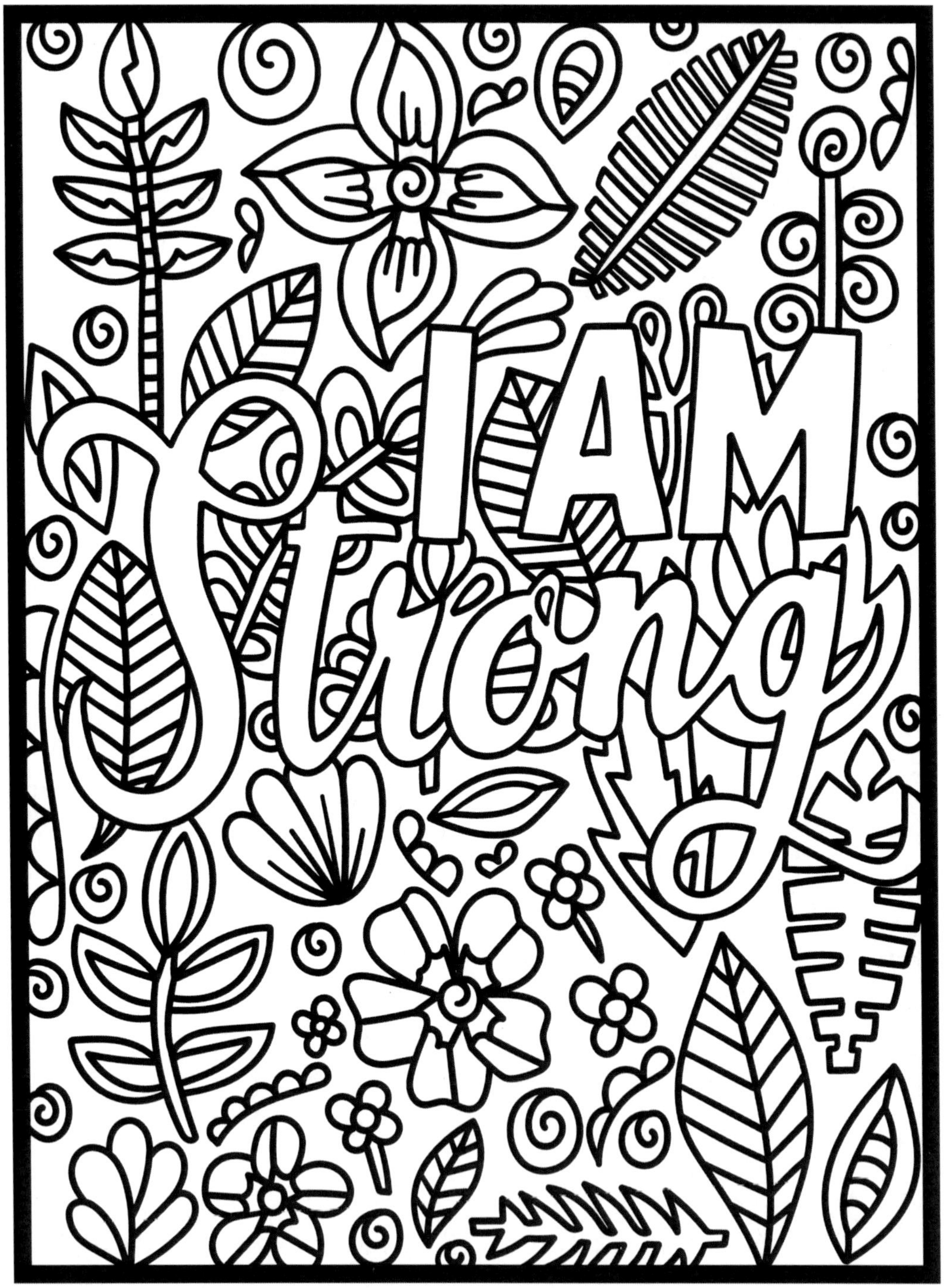
I AM
Strong

BE THE BEST VERSION OF YOURSELF

# DON'T STOP until you're PROUD

# LOVE YOURSELF FIRST

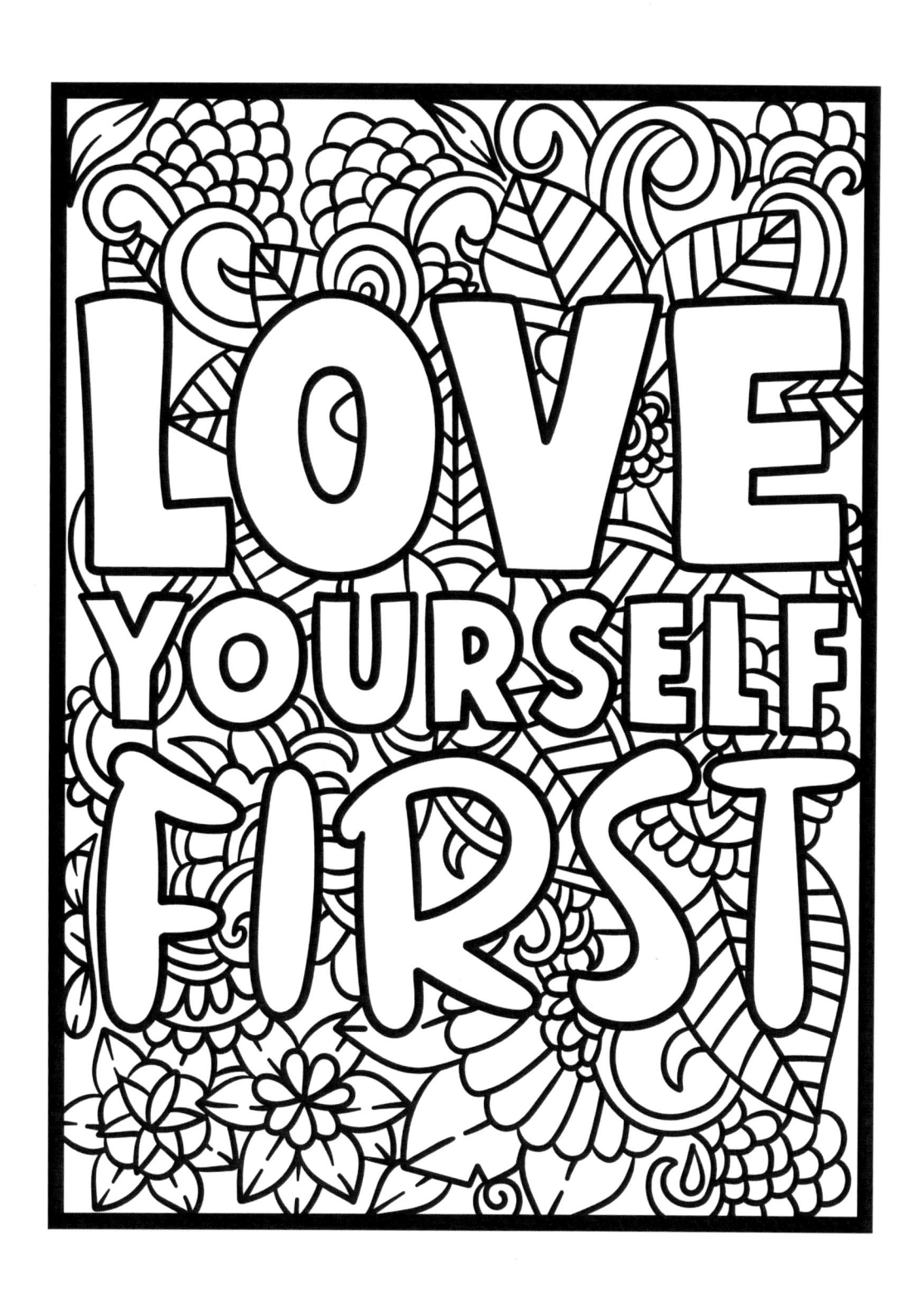

worry less LOVE MORE

ENJOY every MOMENT

LET YOUR HEART SPEAK

DON'T GIVE UP JUST BECAUSE THINGS ARE HARD

Good vibes only

YOU BECOME WHAT YOU BELIEVE

# THINK Positive

# DO AMAZING THINGS

Made in United States
North Haven, CT
26 April 2025